Bold Enough

A Journey from Discouragement to Encouragement

By April C. Mack-Wilson

Edited by Speak Write Play, LLC

ISBN – 978-1-7372138-0-2

Dedication

I first want to thank my heavenly Father, my Daddy, and my Friend. I am nothing without You, and I will always give You all the honor and praise for as long as I have breath in my body. Thank You for giving me a place to belong in Your kingdom and the opportunity to live in freedom.

To the two who have remained constant in my life, my father, Isiah Mack, and my mother, Sandra Mack. I would not be the woman I am today without you two. I am still here! Thank you for your guidance and discipline. Thank you for the opportunities to be the best version of myself. I love you both, and I hope to continue to make you proud.

To my closest friends, you have become my family throughout the years. Thank you for your love, honesty, laughs, hugs, motivation, inspiration, kindness, and for simply being queens as precious as rubies. I love you, my sisters. This one is for us!

To my nursing community, for you all have given me the heart of compassion and desire to serve others as Jesus did. You have helped me grow in my true calling to care. Continue to be strong, be bold, and serve in a capacity that most will never understand.

Finally, to my Grandma Hattie Bell Wilder. You will forever be my inspiration, an example of true love and a woman after God's heart. You were the epitome of "love thy neighbor." I honor you with my words, service to others, and life's purpose. Thank you for blessing me with your love, prayers, encouragement, and faith while on this earth. I now carry your baton of faith to reach future generations. I will forever love you.

Table of Contents

Introduction

Throughout life, how many times have you felt down, discouraged, or even alone in situations? Do you feel as though life knocks you back ten steps as soon as you take one step forward? Do you find that you are the strong friend or family member, so you oftentimes have no one to turn to when you are going through life's challenges? No one to motivate you? No one to simply be available? Do you find it hard to stay encouraged, despite having strong faith in God?

My sister, I understand. You can use my shoulder to cry on, and I will be your listening ear. As you read, you become my listening ear. At the same time, because I went through it, I will also be your safe place against shame, isolation, embarrassment, confusion, or guilt. You are going to walk into a vulnerable, judgment-free zone of inspiration. I believe it is time to be bold enough to walk in freedom.

The conversations you are about to read come from multiple journal entries to myself over time. For years, I have written in journals to lay down my heart, mind, soul, and spirit to God. For years, I wrote my thoughts, frustrations, hurts, fears, concerns, victories, and blessings. When I wrote in my journal, I was often alone and had a lot of questions for God. I felt as though I had no one to talk or turn to. I wrote because I did not think anyone would listen. I wrote because I did not like my own truth. I wrote because I needed clarity. I wrote because, when I finished and tears were often on the pages, God collected them and loved on me.

Reading the Word and journaling have been my sanctuary for encouragement. Many times, writing was my way to try to break out of depression and anxiety. Journaling allowed me to reflect on my day, thoughts, and emotions. It reminded me of my progression in life. Sometimes, when I reread my entries, I feel the moment again or wonder what I was thinking. Other times, I smile and see how God had been orchestrating every detail of my life. He had been preparing me for every desire of my heart—for a life of purpose.

During the COVID-19 pandemic, I realized the need to speak my truth about hope and encouragement. People were hurting, alone, isolated, depressed, and simply trying to make it day by day. As a registered nurse, I witnessed the pains of the pandemic in patients and other healthcare workers, as well as experienced my own struggles with staying strong and navigating complex emotions and thoughts alone. Previous life lessons have taught me to simply keep going, but what do you do when you feel like you cannot make it through another day? Life is hard, and we all need someone to encourage us.

Sister, I hear your heart's cry and know what you are going through. I want you to know that God's Word will uplift you and help you make it through the storms of life. Feeling alone and isolated is something I do not wish on anybody. Feeling anxious and confused all the time can rob you of your peace. Feeling depressed and unloved is a state no one should bear. I desire for everyone to live a life of peace and joy, and I pray that you will see that you do not have to go through your battles alone as you read these pages.

God gives us endurance and encouragement in His Word to stay strong in the faith and deal with the daily pressures of this world. Encouragement is something we all need to keep going, feel motivated, and remain confident in our purpose. God's perfect Word is the source for our true encouragement; it renews us daily.

It's time to be encouraged and stay encouraged, my sister. I aspire to inspire you to be an encouraging force to be reckoned with. In the next seven journal conversations, you will receive the strategies and tools to walk in your own journey of freedom in life. I urge you to strive to live again in the love of God. Remember, the Lord is always with you and at work for your good.

So, let us begin this seven-day encouragement journey together! I fought my biggest battles in seclusion and placed my heart on the pages of the papers and in the hands of God. I now place those pages before you to let you know that you are not alone. In seven days, God created the heavens and the earth. On the seventh day, He rested, and His work was finished. Seven days is all God has given me to share my voice with the world. As you read these conversations, my prayer is that you will understand that God wants to give you the desires of your heart; He will make your plans succeed (Psalm 20:4). You have heard it before, but trust, let go, and let God. He is for you. Let us begin!

Conversation One: Fear Less with God

What I say:

"I can't let fear take over."

What God's Word says:

"For the Spirit God gave us does not make us timid, but gives us power, love and self-discipline" (2 Timothy 1:7).

Fear. I no longer live my life bound by fear, but I mention it in this journey because fear and anxiety were the strongholds that plagued my thoughts and decisions. I allowed fear to take over my mind, spirit, and soul, and that is a dangerous place to settle in life. I now live a life of freedom, love, and a sound mind. I now understand the cost that Jesus paid for my freedom, and I refuse to be a slave to fear.

Reverend Milton Brunson had a song called "I'm Free." The lyrics in the song affirm that someone is free and no longer bound by chains. Well, that is how I feel. But I was not always in this place. If you are ready for a vulnerable moment of honesty, then let us proceed with a few of my fear-filled moments.

One fear-filled moment that immediately darts to the forefront of my mind is when I had to stay longer in basic training after my graduation ceremony because of medical issues. They called it being "a holdover" in basic training. At eighteen years old, the Air Force doctors had to do a biopsy of my cervix. The results sent a surge of emotions through me especially as an eighteen-year-old who was just entering my adulthood life. I felt like life was ending as it was just beginning. While in the military, I continued to get procedures, which left me with the inability to naturally become pregnant. This led to later fears of being inadequate because I may never have a child. Years later, I realized the outcome of that test would forever change my life. Sometimes, I still struggle with this battle of possibly not bearing a child, but I have become content and trust God for His plan for my life.

After leaving the military, I worked for the federal government. I had what others thought was the ideal job and opportunity for growth. I decided to leave the government job to pursue my call to nursing while going through a divorce and wondering how I was going to make it. In this instance, I dealt with two fears. First, there was the fear of surviving by myself and finding a way to make ends meet while going through nursing school—one of the toughest degree programs. Second, I experienced the fear of being divorced, dealing with heartache alone, and feeling judged. I found myself thinking, *Here I am alone again. I've messed up my opportunity to be happily married with a family.* I never had anyone to share my feelings with and simply just pushed through the fear and uncertainty to succeed.

My most recent fear-filled moment started almost two years ago, standing in the rooms of COVID-19 patients. Every time I went to work, I did not know if one day I would be in an ICU bed or cause someone else to be in one. I feared not being adequate or having the experience to take care of certain patients while working as a travel nurse. Ultimately, each patient's life is in my hands. I feared for my own life and health but never expressed it. I woke up before every shift with fear in my heart because it was time to put on my scrubs again. I begged God to give me the strength to get through each shift.

Do you want to know my list of common fears that seem to trouble me sometimes? I have a fear of being broke, judged, and unloved. I fear not being good enough or strong enough. I have a fear of appearing weak, being different, not fitting in, and not receiving approval.

Am I by myself with these fears? It is time to send fear to its grave!

I thought to myself one day, *If I am a child of God, then why am I living a life of fear?* Fear was literally crippling me from living a life of freedom, victory, and purpose. On the outside, I appeared to be fearless. I jumped at opportunities and took leaps of faith that no one else dared to. But my actions stemmed from a place of wanting to do what others expected of me. Therefore, I was trapped in the fear of approval. I was not living in peace even though I claimed to value my peace. The spirit of fear started as a small seed and turned into a growing harvest in my life. It was time to uproot some areas and fertilize the soil with the power of the Holy Spirit. I had to take back what the enemy stole—my peace of mind.

I combatted my fears with the Word of God. The promises of God are true, and everything I had told myself were lies from the enemy. Deuteronomy 31:6-8 says, "Be strong and courageous. Do not be afraid or terrified because of them, for the Lord your God goes with you; He will never leave you nor forsake you." I began to wake up and tell myself that I would have no fear-filled or anxious thoughts. When my heart began to literally pound outside of my chest during an anxious moment, I remembered the Word and told myself that I was not alone because the greatest Helper of all lives within me. Then, I would just keep moving forward in whatever situation I was in.

Our Father goes before us and gives us the strength we need in our moments of weakness. We try to be perfect and walk around as if we will not make mistakes. But since we are not perfect and live in a fallen world, we may make mistakes or decisions we wish we would have thought through better. Guess what? That is okay. We are not perfect, but our God is. Our weaknesses are opportunities for God to show His perfect will in our lives. His grace is sufficient for you, and His power is made perfect in your weakness (2 Corinthians 12:9).

Have you ever felt the loving arms of God wrapped around you? Have you ever encountered the peace and presence of God? When you do (because if you have not but want to, I believe you will because He is always with you), you cannot go back to living in bondage. You must rely on the One who has all the answers.

Recognize who God is in your life and in this world. I place Him in the center of my life and trust His promises. God commands us not to fear. He wants to see us live with purpose. He does not want us to be bound in fear, but He wants us to live in freedom from shame, anxiety, fear, guilt, judgment, past mistakes, insecurities, and doubt.

I let go of all my fears and allowed God to direct my path. Those fearful moments that I mentioned in the beginning of this conversation are a part of my life, but I no longer let them consume me. I made mistakes in the past, but I am not my mistakes. God can still use me, and if you are reading this, I believe that He currently is.

Heart-to-Heart

With every step of your life, know that you are victorious because you have God on your side. You have confidence. You have no fear. Trust that the power of God is working within you. You will not be filled with fear and shrink down in situations that seem impossible. You will rise to every occasion and be filled with the power of the Holy Spirit.

Let God guide you to new heights and depths. He is leading you and supporting you, so you have no reason to fear. It is okay to go running to God whenever a situation becomes too much to bear. He will take you out to the deep, and you will not sink. He is perfect, trustworthy, and a safe place. He is there to help in all situations. You will come out on the winning side!

Journal Release

1. What are your current fears?

2. Have your fears caused you to give up on certain areas in your life?

3. How will faith in God help you endure life's battles of your mind?

4. What are your methods to combat fear? Try focusing on God throughout each day. Reflect on moments when you noticed a change in your thoughts after you focused on God instead of your own fears and anxieties.

Prayer

Dear God,

You have never failed me, and You never will forsake me. In any situation, You are with me. You are faithful, and I trust that I can take courage in your promises when I walk into any situation. Challenges may come, but I will remain strong in Your mighty power. The enemy will not triumph over me. I will stand firm and bold in my faith.

Thank You for working on my behalf. Thank You for Your favor. Thank You for Your divine protection. Help me to remember that no matter what I face or the trials that may come my way, You are always with me. I want to experience Your presence every day, and in every moment of my life. I will rehearse Your truths to sustain and comfort me. In moments when I feel overwhelmed or like life is too much to bear, help me to stay grounded in the foundation of Your strength and promises.

Amen.

Conversation Two: God Has the Ultimate Plan

What I Say:

"Don't worry, I got this!"

What God's Word Says:

> *"Trust in the* LORD *with all your heart and lean not on your own understanding; in all your ways submit to him, and he will make your paths straight"*
> *(Proverbs 3:5-6).*

Has anyone ever said, "Trust me, I got you"? You agree to trust the person, but a small part of you still does not relinquish full control to this person. You say, "Okay." But you still have a desire to guard your heart and subconsciously wait for the individual to prove whether they are completely trustworthy. Maybe this person has failed you in the past, or you have dealt with past hurt from a similar situation. It can be hard to put your full confidence in someone who does not have the best track record of being trustworthy. How can you follow someone and be sure they will not steer you wrong? To prevent a negative outcome or ensure this path is right for you, you find yourself still trying to actively play a role instead of putting your faith in the other person.

Now, how often do you treat God like this? How many times do you pray for something or ask God for His blessing, revelation, or guidance, then take the situation into your own hands? I will be the honest one. I've done that, girl!

I am a sassy little leader, and if anyone knows what is best for me, it must be me. Wrong! God created me for His purposes and His plans. He promised me that "He guides me along the right paths for his name's sake" (Psalm 23:3). However, there have been countless nights where I did not sleep because I was trying to figure out my life and found myself in a whirlwind of thoughts. I spent hours day and night trying to perfectly map out how one decision would impact my entire life. I was not afraid of failing, but since I like to have control over my life, I had to have all the facts and go through every scenario in my head before I made what I thought was the right decision. Talk about high stress, overthinking, and anxiety levels through the roof!

Something about not knowing the outcome of my choices did not sit well with me. What if I make the wrong decision for my life? What if I end up broke? What if I fail? What if I choose the wrong person and end up getting hurt, again? What if the job is too hard or I am not smart enough? I had constant battles in my mind. I was trying to make decisions but could not even trust my own thoughts and reasoning skills.

While putting trust in my own ways, education, finances, wisdom, and understanding, I was slowly opening windows and doors to the enemy. I was allowing him to not only open the doors but also to come in, set up furniture, kick his feet up, and stay for a while. I gave the enemy a comfortable place to reside in my mind simply because I wanted to be in control of my life.

This brings me to another point. Let us talk about missing out on God's will and perfect peace due to constantly worrying and being frustrated. Eventually, my desire for control led me to becoming indecisive and never being consistent with any area of my life. I would start something, then stop in the middle of the project, idea, or plan to pursue something else. I found that I began doubting myself and many of my decisions because I was simply trying to figure it out on my own. This wasn't the way to go because I became more confused and frustrated than ever.

I had to understand the importance of leaning on God because I did not have all the answers, and I never will. I realized that I was putting trust in myself rather than wholeheartedly trusting my Father. I trust in my job, finances, education, experiences, hurts, family, friends, and worldly successes. Why did I have such a hard time putting my trust in God? My biggest problem was that I wanted to be in control of my own life, thoughts, and ways. I wanted God to help me with what I wanted for my life instead of His plan for my life.

The only way I could stop my spiraling thoughts, anxiety, and constant worry was to surrender to Him and place full confidence in the all-powerful and all-knowing God. I had to submit every aspect of my life to His will and allow Him to lead and guide me. You see, I only wanted to trust in what I saw and could control. I gave more weight to what the world said and forgot to focus on the promises of God. This journey of life requires you to trust in the Word and the promises of your Father. You must acknowledge Him and know that He is directing your path.

Including God in every area of your life will keep you on the right path to His promises, riches, and glory. He will guide you. He will not steer you wrong. I let Him into every area, including the dark areas where no light had shone for years. I cried ugly tears, moaned, and groaned because I had no more words to express my pain. I ran out of answers, excuses, strength, and fight. Now that I was empty, vulnerable, and tired of running, God could use me. He was able to fill me, overflow me with His goodness and mercy, and lift me to higher places I never would have imagined. The power of release brings so much peace! Keep on this journey of trust and vulnerability with me. It only gets better.

Heart-to-Heart

Give your Father a heart full of trust every day. Your steps are ordered, and you have been predestined to do the will of God each time you open your eyes. You can surrender your thoughts, mind, decisions, and heart to God. When you feel like you cannot, you must remember how faithful your God is. Combat those negative thoughts with the truth of the Word. Trust your Father's wisdom, for He loves you and has not forgotten about you. He will never fail you. Even in moments that are beyond your control, remember that He is perfectly trustworthy and faithful. When you feel overwhelmed by your circumstances, relinquish control, take a deep breath, and whisper, "God, I trust you."

Journal Release

1. What are you trusting God for today?

2. What does trust in God look like to you?

3. Do you find it hard to trust God because you feel others, or maybe even God, have failed or betrayed you in the past?

4. What barriers are preventing you from completely trusting God with your life? What areas in your life do you need to let go and let God?

Prayer

Dear God,

Help me to trust You in all areas of my life. Help me to let go of areas that I am trying to control. Today, I submit to Your will and Your way. You know what is best for me and exactly what I need to overcome every obstacle that I may face. Help me not to be anxious about anything. But in every situation, by prayer and petition, with thanksgiving, help me to present my requests to You. Guard my heart and mind in Christ Jesus (Philippians 4:6-7). Let everything that I do be for Your glory. Less of me and more of You.

Amen.

Conversation Three: Commit to God to Succeed

What I Say:

"Depend on who? Myself!"

What God's Word Says:

"Commit to the LORD whatever you do, and he will establish your plans"
(Proverbs 16:3).

Commitment means to be dedicated to something. It is a promise to do something. Commitment is often attached to trustworthiness, the act of following through with plans or what you say. As I am writing this, I am also growing and learning in this area. I do not claim to be perfect, but I am constantly evolving and desperately chasing after God's plan for my life.

In the past, committing to anything was a struggle. Do I still have commitment issues? Since I am being completely honest with you, I will say I do in some instances. So, as you continue to read and go through this journey with me, I ask for continued prayers. If this is your weak area, I will pray for you as well. You are not alone. We are on this journey of purpose for the Kingdom together!

Proverbs 16:3 says, "Commit to the Lord whatever you do, and he will establish your plans." I had to dissect this verse so that my mind could understand what my heart already knew. To commit to something means to pledge or entrust oneself to it. I would like to replace "commit" with the word "entrust." When you entrust someone with something, you put that thing into their care and protection. Therefore, committing your works to the Lord means you completely give your works, activities, and daily grind over to God. The next part of the verse says, "and He will establish your plans." In the New King James version it says, "thy thoughts shall be established." Your thoughts should reflect your plans and goals toward your purpose in Christ. God is telling us that those thoughts, our plans, and our purpose will be successful. We are going to win! Therefore, commit to God with complete dependence on Him and have the expectation that there will be an outcome of success.

Often, I find myself entrusting my daily activities to my own strength, schedule, who I am working with on the nightshift, or simply what I hear on the news. I make commitments to things in my life that constantly change and often fail me. I lean on my normal nature of being self-reliant, self-loved, self-dependent, and self-sufficient. These are the characteristics that I have either been taught or learned. But see what they have in common: self. I thought these traits would sustain me until I looked up one day and felt as though I was completely by myself, trying to establish my plans for my life. I began to compare my life to others, looked at what I did not have, and started to think that I was failing in life.

Do you see how quickly my negative mindset took over? I do not know about you, but I want to put my trust and commitment into something that is a sure win. I want the victory in all situations even if the outcome at the time does not look like it will be a success. "We know in all things God works for the good of those who love him, who have been called according to his purpose" (Romans 8:28). Despite what the situation looks like we will get the victory in the end.
Most people usually want to end up on the winning side because no one starts a goal or idea with a plan to fail. We

typically begin a journey with the thought that taking the appropriate steps, having a solid plan and vision, and possessing the knowledge, experience, guidance, and finances will lead us to success when we pull the trigger toward our goals. If things begin to fail, we instantly produce a plan B and begin to navigate through detours to ensure the plan succeeds.

In our efforts to succeed, we take measures into our own hands, and the vision becomes cloudy. Before you know it, you are ready to quit, or you place the plan on hold. Did God get you this far just to leave you high and dry? Absolutely not! He works for us and with us because there are many aspects of this life and beyond this realm that are outside our understanding.

One of my best friends often says to me, "Girl, get out of your own way!" She gets on my nerves when she tells me that because it is usually after I have given her a whole word or dissertation about something in life not going as I planned. Or she says it, after I've been worrying about something I have no control over. Her statement reminds me that I can't be in my own way and try to orchestrate my life instead of entrusting my Father.

The minute I entrust the Lord with every aspect of my life, the daily stressors that used to plague my thoughts become minor. I first had to go to God and ask Him what good works He had for me. I am good at a lot of things. In fact, I do a little of everything well, so many call me a jack of all trades. If you place me in a situation or give me a task, nine times out of ten, I succeed or do it well. Well, I wanted to know what gifts were placed inside of me and what He specifically wanted me to accomplish. I was getting frustrated bouncing around life dabbling in a little of this and that. If I am being honest, I felt like I got a quick thrill by doing something well, then hit a wall and fell into an unfulfilled state. Then, I would find myself with my pen in my journal, feeling frustrated because I could not figure out where I went wrong.

The Message Bible translates Proverbs 16:3 to say, "Put GOD in charge of your work, then what you've planned will take place." The plans that God has for me have been hidden in my heart. They have always been there, but I had to go deeper in my faith, obedience, and intimacy with God to reach them. There was a part of me that had to surrender. The scarred and scared places wanted to keep control; I had lost complete control. I then stopped trying to carry out God's will in my own strength and became desperate for His purpose over my life.

His plans became my plans as I began to seek Him and His approval, not man's approval. To do this, I set aside quality, intimate time with Him to learn His will for my life. What did I realize? He was by my side the entire time. The more I drew near to Him, the more He drew nearer to me. The more I surrendered and trusted God, the more at peace I became with my life and decisions. Now, here I am sharing with you my gift of words of encouragement to help you find the same peace that only God can give.

Heart-to-Heart

Did you know that God wants your plans and goals to succeed? As much as you trust God, He wants to trust you for the assignment He's purposed for you. God is invested in who you will become. Know that your Father wants you to prosper; He wants you to succeed. Let your Father lead and guide you. Walk in the way of the Lord and commit all your works, tasks, and activities unto Him. Get out of your way and simply begin to say, "Thy will be done." Let your response to whatever He reveals to you be, "Yes!"

You are God's masterpiece and were created to do good works (Ephesians 2:10). Rely on God's power to sustain you in moments of weakness. Focus on the plan that your Father has set before you. If God spoke a word to you, it will come to pass. Live with an expectancy of His blessings over your life. Commit everything you do to the Lord and watch your gifts to this world flourish.

Journal Release

1. Do you believe you are living God's plan for your life?

2. Have your plans for your life gone in another direction, or do you feel like it is too late to pursue your original plans? How can you refocus?

3. Have you committed your plans, hopes, and dreams to God?

4. How can you practice involving God in your daily decisions, goals, and plans?

Prayer

Dear God,

I know the plans you have for me will succeed. Help me to stay focused on Your will for my life. As I create goals for my life, I ask for wisdom in making the best decisions. I ask that You continue to stay with me and guide me each day. I will trust You so that I will live out the life You have planned for me. Help me to live a life that aligns with Your plans for me. Keep me in the safe place of Your will. Let all that I do honor You and give You the glory.

Amen.

Conversation Four: Perfect Peace in God

What I Say:

"I cannot control my mental storms."

What God's Word Says:

"You will keep in perfect peace those whose minds are steadfast, because they trust in you" (Isaiah 26:3).

I hate the devil. The enemy is real and comes to steal, kill, and destroy (John 10:10). The enemy has no power over me or any aspect of my life because he has already been defeated. I love God. I am a Christian. I am victorious. I am chosen. I am a daughter of the omnipotent, all-powerful, and all-knowing God. Yes, I know all of this. I believe it. I believe the Word. I believe what God says about me.

I still found myself wondering, *Why do I find myself in mental funks? Is it depression, doubt, or anxiety? Is it adult attention-deficit hyperactivity disorder (ADHD), problems with focusing, or lack of motivation? Is it that I don't have a purpose or haven't found the right job, man, family, or support?* I can ask myself all these questions, but the truth is, I would find myself back in the same place, wondering the same questions year after year.

I was stuck in a cycle. The reality is, I am a smart woman. I excel in school, have three degrees, and pick up tasks quickly. I am a great, compassionate, and caring nurse who performs my calling with excellence. I am intelligent, wise, loyal, respected, and educated, yet I struggle with thoughts of doubt, anxiety, fear, and uncertainty about everything.

Someone recently told me that I am indecisive. Another person cosigned the statement and added, "That's just you. You're all over the place, but we accept it." I could not accept it anymore. I was frustrated with my own mind, and I could not control my thoughts. If I did not regain control, I would continue to spiral into moments of despair and doubt, depression and anxiety, and loneliness and inadequacy.

You see, the devil knows exactly what it takes to keep you right where he wants you. As much as I hate to say it, the devil is smart, cunning, and (most frustrating) patient. A verse to the song "Cycles" by Jonathan McReynolds talks about how the devil pays attention and learns from our mistakes, which is how he is able to keep us going around in cycles. (Are you singing the song with me? Because I almost forgot I was typing and started focusing on the song. This mind of mine!) The devil has had it out for me since I was young, and he won't quit. The enemy knows your potential, so he tries to prevent you from being all that God has created you to be.

God has kept me in many situations. I think of numerous situations and wonder how I am still here on this earth. I recall having experiences with the wrong people and being in the wrong places, but I somehow made it out at the right times. Sometimes, I was aware of the attacks of the enemy, but other times, they were so subtle that I wouldn't even call them "attacks." I have felt the darkness of the enemy in rooms, and I have encountered him in dreams.

I let the devil get into my mind to the point of almost no return. In some cases, the sin I committed was so small that I would brush it off and make an excuse. Excuses literally almost became the death of me. In other cases, I allowed the enemy to convince me that my life had no purpose and that the best option was to end it all. One morning after mixing pills with alcohol the night before, I found myself waking up to emergency medical service workers at my door. I was still alive, but I found myself sitting in a psychiatric facility and realizing the person I had become was not who God said I was. I was in a dark place, but God was my light in the dark. Yes, the enemy literally tried to take me out. I will discuss more about this valley in the end.

I remember listening to a sermon by Stephanie Ike while driving to a travel nurse assignment one day. In the message, she said God gives us revelations in our Spirits, but our minds can be so unhealthy that we cannot activate them.[1] Whew! Honey, I don't know about you, but I am trying to receive every spiritual blessing that God has for me. Therefore, I had to dive into destroying the stronghold of my own mind. At the time, my mind was what I would now call "unhealthy," but I was in denial back then. I consistently filled my mind with doubt, fear, uncertainty, feelings of inadequacy, and depressive thoughts. I found myself in a "funk" often, but I knew it wasn't a normal funk.

You see, I know when I am under attack. I know when the enemy is telling me lies, and I even know when I have done something to open the door to him. You would think I would be smarter than that. I am. But the reality is that it was my inconsistency in life and dependence on my flesh that kept placing me in those situations. You see, when your mind is not healthy, the spiritual blessings God has for you cannot be activated.

In one journal entry, I wrote three things that I may have gotten from a past sermon or devotional text. It's also possible the words were spoken to me, so I do not claim them as original thoughts. But I want to share the importance of God's peace:

1. God's peace is permanent and secure.
2. God's peace is found in the midst of chaos.
3. God's peace does not change with the circumstances.

I desired God's peace of mind in my life, and only my heavenly Father could provide it. Isaiah 26:3 says, "You will keep in perfect peace those whose minds are steadfast, because they trust in you". The Message Bible says, "People with their minds set on you, you keep completely whole, Steady on their feet, because they keep at it and don't quit" (Isaiah 26:3). Colossians 3:2 states, "Set your minds on things above, not on earthly things". According to God's Word, how do I gain control of my mind? I keep it set on God.

Heart-to-Heart

End your search for finding peace in the world because what you desire is a peace that surpasses understanding. With this peace, you will remain calm in the midst of the storm because your Father is with you. You may face trials and tribulations that will bring you stress, anxiety, and confusion. In those moments, keep your eyes and mind focused on your Father. He will keep you in perfect peace if you stay focused on Him instead of the situation at hand.

If one day gets a little crazy and turns into weeks and months of craziness that cause you to begin to feel overwhelmed, simply ask your Father to refocus your mind on Him. Call on Him as many times as you need to throughout the day. There is something precious about the name of Jesus. He will help you to make it through each moment of your day. Remain in perfect harmony with your Father. You are His child, and the racing thoughts are nothing but a scheme concocted by the enemy to keep you bound. Be free in your mind and keep God's words hidden in your heart.

Journal Release

1. Are you causing your own storms in your life? What situations do you need to give to God and stop worrying about?

2. How can you stay in a place of peace during tough times?

3. Is your mind in a good place right now?

4. What do you need God to heal you from to maintain your peace?

Prayer

Dear God,

Protect my mind and thoughts against the enemy. I pray for Your perfect peace that can only be found when I trust in You. Let my faith be unwavering when the ways of the world become too much for me to bear. Help me meditate on the promises of Your Word and Your unfailing love. Let my mind stay focused on things above. Let me think on whatever is true, noble, right, pure, lovely, and admirable (Philippians 4:8). You love me, and you are a good Father. Keep my mind staid on You.

Amen.

Conversation Five: Fearfully and Wonderfully Made

What I Say:

"Image issues? I have them."

What God's Word Says:

> *"For you created my inmost being; you knit me together in my mother's womb. I praise you because I am fearfully and wonderfully made; your works are wonderful, I know that full well"*
> *(Psalm 139:13-14).*

My goal in life is to look more and more like my heavenly Father. The Bible says that we are created in His image (Genesis 1:26-27). Romans 8:29 says, "For those God foreknew he also predestined to be conformed to the image of his Son," so I am on a mission to learn who I am in Christ. In a world that has strayed so far from the image of God, I choose to continue to reflect my Father. I choose to be a woman of spiritual beauty—beauty that is timeless and radiates from the inside.

Look in the mirror. Do you realize that your Father created you just the way you are, on purpose and for a purpose? You were created by God to do His good works throughout the world, and you can have confidence in knowing that He will fulfill His promises through you. God created you in your mother's womb and loved you from the beginning.

God knows us better than we know ourselves. He knows the number of hairs on our heads, our thoughts before we think them, and the ultimate reasons why we were created. Just sit for a moment and think about God creating you with His hands. Reflect for a minute on the fact you have been *handcrafted* by God Himself. Nothing about how you were created is random or by accident. The Creator of all things found the importance and need for *you* in this world.

Why are we so unhappy with ourselves, how we look, think, and the talents or gifts we don't have? Why do we compare ourselves to others rather than celebrating our differences and individual gifts? You may give me the side eye for what I'm about to say, but thank God for the free will He gives. We can choose what to read and what we allow to enter our minds. So here goes nothing!

The media has changed how we view ourselves. Many of us look at ourselves and think we are too short, skinny, or too fat. We think our lips should be fuller, behinds bigger, and stomachs flatter. We constantly want to change something on the outside, but how determined are we to change the inside? In one moment, without a thought, we will go and inject our bodies with who knows what or cut off and add to ourselves. What about cutting off negativity, toxic people, bad behaviors, and generational curses? What about injecting our minds, emotions, and souls with the truth of the Word that will set us free from the bondage of this world?

I am not judging those who get work done on their bodies to make themselves happy or feel beautiful. I, too, look in the mirror and see my flaws. Many times, after scrolling through social media, I have torn myself to shreds because I was insecure about how I looked. I used to hate leaving the house without makeup on because I was self-conscious about my acne marks. There was even a time when I tried multiple procedures to get rid of my cellulite, which I now just accept and poke at from time to time. If I am being completely honest, which I am, I contacted a medical spa recently to work on my stomach because I want to eat what I want and not work out. I am tired of working out most days after working back-to-back night shifts! I do not judge you, my sister, so do not judge me. We are all in this together.

Let's get back to the true essence of our beauty, worth, and love for ourselves. The light and Spirit of God that is within us radiates an image of God, which is where our true beauty comes from. Psalm 34:5 says, "Those who look to him are radiant, their faces are never covered with shame." I want us to get back to being full of peace, showing patience, demonstrating kindness, reflecting goodness, displaying faithfulness, exuding gentleness, and exercising self-control (Galatians 5:22-23). Let us realize that we were created for a purpose.

God had us in mind from the very beginning to bear His image (Genesis 1:27). An image is a reflection of something or someone. If God created us in His image, then our purpose is already within. Stop stifling your purpose as an image bearer of Christ by trying to be and look like everyone else. Reflect the purposeful greatness that is already within you. (This is a message for you and me because I am a self-proclaimed certified social media scroller.) Stop idolizing the world's standards of beauty and worth because, believe me, they will change in a few months. Begin to keep your eyes on the One who is always constant and never changing, our Father.

Heart-to-Heart

You are unique, and there is no other person in the world just like you. You are an original. God has numbered the hairs on your head and created you in His amazing image. Thank your Father for all body systems that intricately work together to form who you are. Do not dwell on your weaknesses, for God's power is made perfect in your weaknesses (2 Corinthians 12:9).

Walk in your purpose because *you* are special. *You* are as rare as rubies. *You* are needed. *You* are handcrafted by God. Stop criticizing yourself, downplaying your abilities, comparing yourself to others, and being so hard on yourself. Praise your Father and know that He does not make mistakes. Fix your crown, for you are chosen, God's special possession. You are His masterpiece. Let no one take that away from you.

Just in case no one told you today, **you are beautiful**, my sister, and I love you!

Journal Release

1. When you look in the mirror, what do you see? Do you see who you really are?

2. What do you say about yourself daily? Are your thoughts about yourself positive or negative?

3. What can you do to appreciate your flaws and weaknesses and see yourself as God sees you?

4. Is God pleased with how you represent yourself for His kingdom?

Prayer

Dear God,

Thank You for choosing to create me. Thank You for giving me life. Thank You for the gifts, talents, and abilities that You placed within me. You have been better to me than I have been to myself. Help me to remind myself that my flaws and weaknesses do not define me. In fact, You know my weaknesses and can still use them for Your glory. You know me inside and out, and I praise You for the way You made me in Your image. Search my heart so that I will continue to become more like You. I have worth in You, and I will embrace this daily. Teach me to live the life You intended for me despite what the world says. I will follow Your standards, not the standards of the world. I will keep You first for I am nothing without You.

Amen.

Conversation Six: Do Not Be Anxious

What I Say:

"Anxiety must go!"

What God Says:

"Therefore do not worry about tomorrow, for tomorrow will worry about itself. Each day has enough trouble of its own"
(Matthew 6:34).

Don't worry. Be happy! Worry is one of my biggest enemies. However, worry has never changed any situation. Constant worry is a worthless seed that we give water to until it grows and takes over our minds. Being anxious and worrying about life is worthless; it wastes so much time and energy.

Do not let worry control your future. When you worry, you are telling God that He cannot take care of your problems. You are saying to Him that He does not have the answers. You are telling God that He is not in control. Do you remember that song titled "He's Got the Whole World in His Hands"? Was it just a song, or do you believe that He truly has the entire world in His hands?

I believe God is in control; however, I still woke up each morning in deep anxiety as I thought about everything I had to do. I woke up thinking about work, the tasks on my to-do list, the possible events of the next day, what I was going to wear, whether I needed gas in my car, and what I needed to cook and do meal prep. The list is endless. Since I am a single woman, I carried the weight of the world to accomplish all the tasks by myself.

The root of my anxiety stemmed from my reliance on myself. We are to rely on God, not ourselves. This mindset is completely countercultural. Everything in society seems to be about self-love, self-empowerment, and independence. *Look at me! Look what I did! Look where I am going! Me, me, me.* We promote ourselves in a manner that makes us think we are the reason for everything that occurs in our lives. Yes, I work hard, save, make plans, make decisions, and live my life. However, God wakes me up each day. He blesses me with my gifts, health, mind, and voice. He orchestrates my life, and for that reason alone, I can wake up and not be anxious.

We are to live with the hope and certainty that our Father in heaven is in full control of our lives. I am not telling you to not prepare and set goals for the future. I am simply saying to do it without the constant worry because that can soon turn into anxiety. If I have learned nothing else on this journey, it is that I will make mistakes. Making the wrong decisions and acting before God intended led to me taking steps backwards. There is no situation that is too big or too hard for our God. Take your concerns to God in prayer and ask Him to bring clarity and peace to you about the situation you're dealing with. Ask God to help you live your life with a dependency on Him.

I would like to share one of my journal entries from May 2, 2020. God told me:

> My daughter, during this time, I am teaching you to live totally dependent on Me, not your emotions, circumstances, people, mate, or the

> world. You are to rely on Me. You feel alone, but in those times, come to Me. I will take away loneliness. You feel tired; I will give you the strength and rest you need. You feel frustrated; I will give you clarity, knowledge, and understanding. Stop trying to be Miss Independent with Me. You cannot do it on your own. I did not create you to navigate this world by yourself. I left you with my Holy Spirit to guide you and prepare you for what I have next for you. Please just be my daughter. I know what is best for you. Stop feeling disappointed and worrying. Stop comparing your life to others. I know your path. I prepared it before I created you. I created you specifically for the purpose I am preparing you for. Trust Me. Follow My commands. Turn to Me. Obey Me. I am your Father in heaven, and I love you.

As God spoke to me, it served as a reminder that He is always with me. He is close to me. He cares. He never intended for me to try navigating through this life by myself. He desires for me to go to Him and seek Him. Matthew 6:33 says, "But seek first his kingdom and his righteousness, and all these things will be given to you as well." Seek the kingdom of God first and know that He is in full control. God will give you freedom and peace in the middle of any situation.

Refocus your thoughts on whatever is true, noble, right, pure, lovely, admirable, excellent, and praiseworthy (Philippians 4:8). When you tell yourself not to think about something, what do you do? You think about it. I began refocusing my mind on positive thoughts and on the promises of God.

Focus on today and do not worry about what tomorrow may hold.

Heart-to-Heart

Live for the day that your Father has placed before you. Do not let the fear or anxiety of tomorrow rob you of today's joys and blessings. Anxiety and worry get you nowhere. Cast all your cares on Him and put your life in the unchanging hands of your Father. Instead of carrying anxious burdens, hand the situation over to your Father. Pray and seek the kingdom of God. Then, because you belong to Christ Jesus, God will bless you with peace that no one can completely understand. And this peace will control the way you think and feel. He knows what tomorrow holds, so you can have full confidence in knowing that He will meet all your needs today, tomorrow, and forever. Your Father is with you now. Enjoy the wonderous glory and presence of God today.

Journal Release

1. What is giving you anxiety right now?

2. Does your anxiety cause you to make impulsive decisions or leave you stuck when you should be moving forward?

3. Why do you have so much anxiety when you trust God?

4. In what area of your life do you need increased faith?

Prayer

Dear God,

I pray over my daily thoughts. Father, guard my heart and mind. I worry and oftentimes get frustrated when things do not go as planned. Deliver me from my fears and moments filled with doubt and worry. I trust You. I know that no aspect of my life is hidden from You or occurs without You knowing. You are my everything. You are my peace, joy and hope for today and tomorrow. I will remain confident in Your promises and dwell in Your presence. I will pray about every situation and present my requests to You.

Amen.

Conversation Seven: You Have a Hope and a Future

What I Say:

"I want to end it all!"

What God's Word Says:

"'For I know the plans I have for you,' declares the LORD, 'plans to prosper you and not to harm you, plans to give you hope and a future'"
(Jeremiah 29:11).

How was your day? How many times have you been asked this question and managed to muster the strength to say, "I'm good," even though you were completely falling apart on the inside? You were dealing with health issues, divorce, feeling alone, kids, pain, feelings of abandonment, isolation, generational curses, inadequacy, and more. Despite this, you still managed to tell the other person that you were fine. But in your mind, you were steadily thinking, *What am I going to do with my life? How can God use a person like me? God created me on purpose, yet I still somehow managed to create a mess with my life.*

You see, I have had secret struggles that I have battled completely alone because I thought I didn't have any options. I deployed to Afghanistan from 2009-2010. After my deployment, I found myself in a very dark place and had a hard time adjusting to returning home. I worked in the ICU in Afghanistan, and I also deployed to an Army forward operating base. I did not realize how I was affected until I returned from deployment. I was diagnosed with posttraumatic stress disorder (PTSD), anxiety, depression, and alcohol abuse. I struggled with excessive drinking and took prescription medications after my military deployment. I found myself in such a dark place. In February 2009, I tried to take my life, but gratefully, I am here to tell the story. I will say that I have not contemplated suicide since the day I mentioned in a previous conversation when I mixed prescription pills with alcohol. But I often wonder why I am on this earth. I am a true believer in the words of Paul in Philippians 1:6 when he says, "Being confident of this, that he who began a good work in you will carry it on to completion until the day of Christ Jesus." My time on this earth is not finished, and I am confident that I will complete what God started within me. I have a future, and there is work to be done on this earth for the kingdom of God.

So, I write these words for you to read so that you will know that you are not alone. There is hope in knowing that you are loved. You are here for a purpose—on purpose. Nothing in this life is too hard for God. You do not have to face your trials by yourself.

I faced many of my hardships alone in very dark moments. Looking back, I realize the devil wanted me to stay in those dark places and make me believe I was alone. When the enemy gets you by yourself, especially when you are trying to handle your emotions and situations on your own, you are almost defenseless. Therefore, you need to ask God to send the right people in your life to encourage you. You need people who will stand in prayer for you when you do not have the faith or energy to do so for yourself. Most importantly, you need our perfect God to save and work in your innermost being.

One of my favorite scripture verses is Jeremiah 29:11: "'For I know the plans I have for you,' declares the Lord, 'plans to prosper you and not to harm you, plans to give you a hope and a future.'" I held onto this scripture with my life because its words gave me the peace and hope I needed to get through some of my darkest moments. We have a hope in God that our lives are in His hands. He has a plan on this earth, and to fulfill this plan, we must live in Him. Second, we must understand that trials will come our way because we live in a fallen world. Just because we are followers of Christ does not make us exempt from the conflicts, sufferings, hurts, and brokenness of this world. But what we do have is the Almighty God, who helps us persevere through them. He will keep us strong in our weaknesses and covered when the enemy rages war all around us.

No matter what happens in our lives, we can persevere and experience victory in Christ. We have the option to keep our eyes on Him and His vision for our lives rather than abandon hope and give up. We can rejoice in our sufferings because we know that they produce perseverance, character, and hope (Romans 5:3-5). In everything we do in our lives, we have a hope that does not put us to shame.

I don't know about you, but I have had many moments in my life when I wanted to put my head in the sand and disappear. But God said, "Not yet." So, if nothing else gives you hope, know that God has never and will never take His hand off your life.

I want you to remember that God has a plan and purpose for your life. Maybe you are not exactly where you want to be in life, or maybe you are in a season of difficulty and even questioning your purpose. Regardless of where you are right now, your Father thinks about you. You are always on His mind. He knows what He has in store for you on the exact day, in the exact hour, and at the exact minute. You are continuously in His thoughts. Trust Him, for His ways and thoughts are higher than this earth (Isaiah 55:8-9). He sits high in the heavens as your Father and your Friend, waiting to bless you exceedingly and abundantly (Ephesians 3:20). This is only the beginning of what your Father has in store for you. Live today and each day knowing that your Father has promised a great future for you. Lean on the hope and promises of your Father. He is faithful and a firm foundation during any situation. Believe that His promises will surely come to pass in your life.

Your story is not over, my sister. If you are still here, you have a purpose. He has a plan for you. Suicide is not the answer. You are a precious jewel in the eyes of your Father, and He loves you. Guess what? I love you too, my sister, and I need you here to do what no one else on this earth can.

Heart-to-Heart

Do not be discouraged or frustrated. Do not feel like you do not measure up to the world's expectations. Your Father will carry out the good works He has prepared you to do. Submit to His will and His leading. Remain in Him, and He will remain in you. God sees where you are. God sees *you.* He placed something amazing in you that must be shared with the world. Have no doubts about the promises of God. Put your faith in the confidence of God. He created you for His purposes, and He always finishes what He begins. Stay in the will of your Father and remain connected to the source of your life. You are God's workmanship, and He will do great things through you. Rest in your Father's capable hands.

Journal Release

1. What has God promised you about your future? What promises can you focus on today?

2. How does focusing your mind on God's promises help you stay positive and get through the day?

3. What do you believe is your life's purpose?

4. Do you have someone or a group you can confide in when you are feeling down? Find a place or a person to get connected to.

Prayer

Dear God,

Sometimes I feel like quitting and giving up. I often wonder if I am going in the right direction or if I completely missed the mark in life. Father, guide me to develop my gifts and talents. Show me the purpose for my life. Work on my heart and mind and give me assurance that You will perfect and complete the good works You placed within me. You are faithful, and You have promised to always be with me. Help me to continue to speak Your promises daily in faith. Teach me to meditate and focus my mind on trusting Your ways and plans for my life. Keep my mind and teach me to walk in alignment with Your will.

Amen.

Conclusion

I have written my entire life and never knew it would lead to others reading the words that God so often placed on my heart. I began to write in my journals as a source of therapy and healing. The following passage is from Sunday, June 30, 2013:

> As I begin to write, I don't know the purpose of it or what may come to pass as I put pen to paper. I don't know if this is going to be a story of my personal experiences each day or my spiritual journey or just thoughts that get me through life. I just felt like writing. I pray that, as I write, God will begin to guide my pen. I pray that, through my writing, I will be able to gain a closer relationship with Him. I have lately struggled with purpose and uncertainty. I have begun to wonder what more is in store for me.
>
> Last night, I read Romans 8:28, which says, "And we know that in all things God works for the good of those who love him, who have been called according to his purpose." Purpose. This is what I struggle with. When you doubt your purpose or have unanswered questions regarding your purpose, you begin to lose sight of your life. If you don't know what your purpose is, how do you know what direction to take? Who to talk to? Where to go? What to do? When to do it? I can go on and on.
>
> The only way to discover your true purpose is to go to God. He is my creator, and He holds the master plan to my life. So, as I question certain aspects of

> my life and grow tired of trying to figure it out on my own, I find that it must be time (it's actually overdue) to truly learn how to seek God and have the relationship that I know I need. Lord, I ask that You help me find the areas in my life that can be used for Your purpose.

Today, September 12, 2021, I am currently writing the final chapter of what I like to call "my journal conversations." As you read this final chapter, I believe that God is going to bring restoration to all areas of your life. I believe God wants to work through you to show others how good He is and how much He truly cares for and loves His children.

He wants the best for you; however, you must seek Him first. You must keep your eyes on Him. No matter the situation, good or bad, keep your eyes on God. Begin to focus on the good, despite how you feel.

Remember that everything you go through is all part of His purpose for your life. Begin to ask God what He is trying to tell or show you in the tough situations or places you find yourself in. Let God be the center of everything. Understand that these lessons are for what God has in store for you.

Say this with me: I know God loves me. I want to be one of His children that He can depend on—a child whom He is willing to provide for because, in the end, it will give Him glory. God, let Your will be done. I pray for restoration in all areas of my life. Less of me and more of You. Use me, mold me, and shape me. I am Your workmanship. I lack nothing, for You will provide. You know what I need even before I ask. You know what it takes to prepare me for the next level.

I will always be on top; I will be the head and not the tail if I continue to follow Your commands.

As you continue to follow the ways of the Lord, you're going to come back better than before. God is behind the scenes working everything out in your favor! Be bold enough to live a life of encouragement, instead of discouragement, and watch God work!

Scriptures for the Mind

These are verses I often reference when battling negative thoughts in my mind. I hope you find comfort in the Word as much as I do.

2 Corinthians 10:4-5

"The weapons we fight with are not the weapons of the world. On the contrary, they have divine power to demolish strongholds. We demolish arguments and every pretension that sets itself up against the knowledge of God, and we take captive every thought to make it obedient to Christ."

John 10:10

"The thief comes only to steal and kill and destroy; I have come that they may have life, and have it to the full."

James 4:7

"Submit yourselves, then, to God. Resist the devil, and he will flee from you."

Romans 12:2

"Do not conform to the pattern of this world, but be transformed by the renewing of your mind. Then you will be able to test and approve what God's will is—his good, pleasing and perfect will."

Psalm 34:17

"The righteous cry out, and the Lord hears them; he delivers them from all their troubles."

Psalm 91:1-4

"Whoever dwells in the shelter of the Most High will rest in the shadow of the Almighty. I will say of the Lord, 'He is my refuge and my fortress, my God, in whom I trust.' Surely he will save you from the fowler's snare and from the deadly pestilence. He will cover you with his feathers, and under his wings you will find refuge; his faithfulness will be your shield and rampart."

Psalm 55:22

"Cast your cares on the LORD and he will sustain you; he will never let the righteous be shaken."

2 Timothy 4:18

"The Lord will rescue me from every evil attack and will bring me safely to his heavenly kingdom. To him be glory for ever and ever. Amen."

Proverbs 3:5-6

"Trust in the LORD with all your heart and lean not on your own understanding; in all your ways submit to him, and he will make your paths straight."

Philippians 4:8

"Finally, brothers and sisters, whatever is true, whatever is noble, whatever is right, whatever is pure, whatever is lovely, whatever is admirable—if anything is excellent or praiseworthy—think about such things."

Jeremiah 29:11

"'For I know the plans I have for you,' declares the LORD, 'plans to prosper you and not to harm you, plans to give you hope and a future.'"

About the Author

April Mack-Wilson is a compassionate servant and woman after God's heart. She is God-fearing, faith-filled, obedient, and always ready and willing to do God's work. She is a registered nurse and has been in the healthcare field for almost twenty years. She is a veteran and served as a medic in the United States Air Force. April holds a Bachelor of Science in Health Administration, a Bachelor of Science in Nursing, and a Master of Public Health. She is a member of Sigma Theta Alpha Military Sorority, Inc.

Dubbed the "Bedside Hope Dealer," April loves caring for others in the healthcare field and throughout the community. She shares her gift of caregiving and works to be an example of God's way to overall wellness. She focuses on her purpose to serve in the lives of people who need hope, faith, and encouragement in difficult times. April believes God has a unique purpose for each person and aspires to be a living example of God's glory for those who need a gentle reminder.

In her spare time, April enjoys working out, eating, and spending time with loved ones who make her laugh and feed her soul with joy.

Note

1. Ike, Stephanie, "Help! My Mind Is A Mess," (sermon), ONE A Potter's House Church, YouTube video, Feb 5, 2021, https://www.youtube.com/watch?v=_QEtiRNlwSc.

Made in the USA
Coppell, TX
12 July 2022